WEEKLY **WR** READER®
EARLY LEARNING LI

This Is My Story

I Come from India

by Valerie J. Weber

Reading consultant: Susan Nations, M.Ed., author/literacy coach/
consultant in literacy development

Please visit our web site at: www.garethstevens.com
For a free color catalog describing Weekly Reader® Early Learning Library's list
of high-quality books, call 1-877-445-5824 (USA) or 1-800-387-3178 (Canada).
Weekly Reader® Early Learning Library's fax: (414) 336-0164.

Library of Congress Cataloging-in-Publication Data

Weber, Valerie.
   I come from India / by Valerie J. Weber.
     p. cm. — (This is my story)
   Includes bibliographical references and index.
     ISBN-10: 0-8368-7235-5 — ISBN-13: 978-0-8368-7235-4 (lib. bdg.)
     ISBN-10: 0-8368-7242-8 — ISBN-13: 978-0-8368-7242-2 (softcover)
    1. East Indian Americans—Social life and customs—Juvenile literature.   2. Immigrant children—
United States—Juvenile literature.   3. Immigrants—United States—Juvenile literature.
4. Hyderabad (India)—Social life and customs—Juvenile literature.   5. India—Social life and customs—
Juvenile literature.   6. United States—Social life and customs--Juvenile literature.   I. Title.
   E184.E2W43   2007
   973'.0491411—dc22   2006018404

This edition first published in 2007 by
Weekly Reader® Early Learning Library
A Member of the WRC Media Family of Companies
330 West Olive Street, Suite 100
Milwaukee, WI 53212 USA

Art direction: Tammy West
Cover design, page layout, and maps: Charlie Dahl

Photography: All photos © John Sibilski Photography, except page 13, © Ted Streshinsky/CORBIS

Printed in the United States of America

1 2 3 4 5 6 7 8 9 10 09 08 07 06

Table of Contents

Cover and title page: I go to school in Wisconsin now, but I started learning English in school in India.

Life in Big Countries

Hi! My name is Suhith. My family left India when I was six years old and moved to the United States. We live near Milwaukee, Wisconsin.

The United States is three times as big as India, but India has many more people. In fact, China is the only country in the world with more people than India!

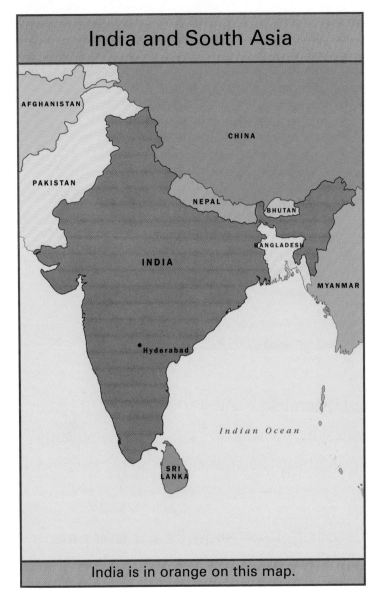

India and South Asia

AFGHANISTAN

CHINA

PAKISTAN

NEPAL

BHUTAN

BANGLADESH

INDIA

MYANMAR

Hyderabad

Indian Ocean

SRI LANKA

India is in orange on this map.

India is huge — big enough to be called a subcontinent. Subcontinent means that it is a large area of land that is smaller than a **continent**. India stretches from the Himalaya Mountains in the north to the Indian Ocean in the south.

India also has forests, deserts, beaches, lakes, and grasslands. I lived in **Hyderabad** (HI-duh-ruh-bad), a busy, modern city.

5

I never saw snow like this in India!

It can get very hot in Hyderabad — over 100 **degrees**! I liked the weather there, even when it was so hot. When the rainy season began and it rained for the first time, the air smelled wet and good.

When I moved to Wisconsin, I saw snow for the first time. I like playing in the snow. I do not like how cold it gets here, though!

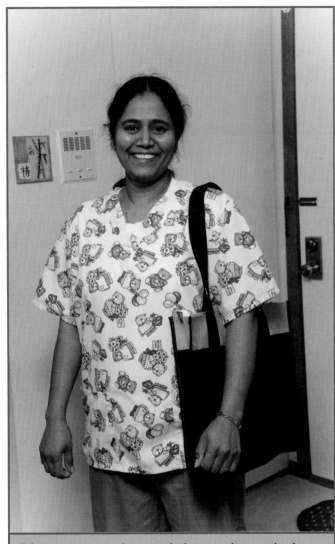

My mom works at night, and my dad takes care of me and my sister.

My mother is a nurse. She works in a hospital unit where babies are born. She trained to be a nurse in India. She heard about jobs for nurses in Wisconsin, so we came here.

Our apartment building has three stories.

There are many differences between my home in India and my home here. In India, my house was very big. I could play on the flat roof on top of the first story, or level. Sometimes our family went up to the roof to sit at nighttime. We could hear the noises of the city.

Now we live in an apartment. No one can play or sit on the roof.

This is my family. My sister is nineteen. She goes to college.

We lived with my grandparents in India. I liked living with them, and I still miss them. They want to come visit us here. In Wisconsin, I live with my mother, father, and sister.

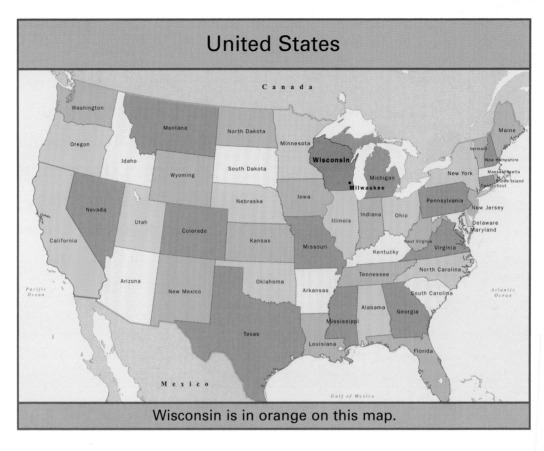

United States

Wisconsin is in orange on this map.

Milwaukee is the largest city in Wisconsin. It has half a million people. More than six million people live in Hyderabad in India.

Food and Faith

I liked all kinds of food in India, but I especially liked dosas (DOE-sahs). These are flat pancakes made from rice and **lentil** flour.

I never tasted pizza until I came to the United States. It is so good! The first time I ate macaroni and cheese, I did not like it. I put sugar on it, and it tasted much better!

My mom is teaching me how to make dosas. It is hard to flip them over at just the right time.

This is a special dinner for us. My mom is wearing her **traditional** Indian dress.

We eat many of the same foods here as we did in India. We can get the **ingredients** at many grocery stores.

Stores are very different here than in India. In Hyderabad, we used to shop at a large market with many **stalls**. Each stall sold different items. Some sold spices, and some sold vegetables. We bought fruit at a different stall.

Statues like this one stand in Hindu temples in India and the United States.

We are **Hindus**. **Hinduism** is the world's third largest religion. It is over six thousand years old.

In India, many people around us followed the same faith. When we lived in India, our temple was only a block away. In the United States, we have to go much farther to worship with other people. We have to drive more than half an hour to go to **temple** in a small town nearby.

Life in School

I go to a small school near Milwaukee. My class has about twenty-three kids. In India, I had fewer children in my class. My school was unusual, however. In most city schools in India, teachers have about forty children in their class.

My teacher and I talk about my book for my book report. I really liked reading *The Chronicles of Narnia*.

My friend and I are learning **sign language** and Spanish at the same time.

We did not wear jeans and sweatshirts to school in India. We wore uniforms instead. As we moved from grade to grade, the color of our uniforms changed.

I do not know whether I like uniforms or being able to choose my clothes. My mother liked us in uniforms, though. No one could argue about what to wear in the morning!

I have lots of friends in school. I do not like leaving anyone out. I do not want to hurt anyone's feelings.

Some of my friends are from other countries, too! One friend's family came from Russia.

We are learning about different rhythms in music class. We can also try out different instruments. I have played a **xylophone** and a **tambourine**. I like music from India, too, especially rap and rock.

I was chosen to play the tambourine, the best instrument in music class!

Fun at Home

I practice my violin at home. I also like to play in different sports. When I was seven, I started playing soccer. I also learned how to swim and play basketball.

In India, I used to play cricket. As in baseball, players use a ball and bat in this game. The bat is shaped like a paddle. Many children play cricket in India.

I started playing the violin four months ago. I practice fifteen minutes every day.

In India, I played with toys and saw a ton of videos. I watched those every day. I also made up different games using sticks and ropes.

I like playing video games at home.

Many people think the game of chess was invented in India.

Sometimes I play different games with my sister. We like to play chess, but she always beats me! I also play with my gerbil named Max. I had two pets when I lived in India. One was a dog named Bingo, and the other was a goldfish.

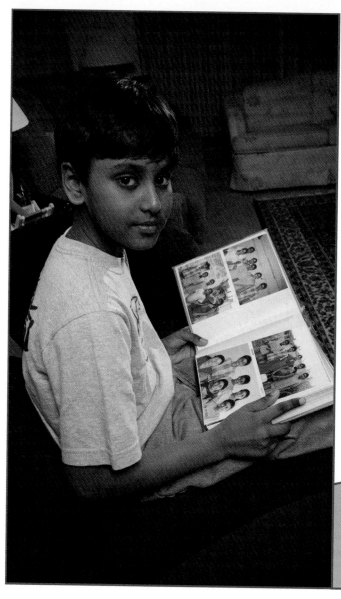

I like both India and Milwaukee, but I miss my family in India. My grandparents, aunts, uncles, and cousins live there still. I wish we could see them someday.

I like looking at photos of our family in India. They remind me of my first home.

Glossary

continent — one of the large land masses of the world. Earth has seven continents.

degrees — units for measuring temperature

Hinduism — a religion in which followers believe in one God, who appears in many different forms

Hindus — followers of the Hindu religion

Hyderabad — a city in central India that is the capital of the state of Andhra Pradesh

ingredients — items that something is made from

lentil — a flat seed like a bean

sign language — a language that uses hand movements to communicate

stalls — counters or booths where things are displayed to be sold

tambourine — a small drum with metal disks attached to the side

temple — a building that people worship in

traditional — based on custom or an older fashion

xylophone — a musical instrument with wooden bars of different lengths that make different sounds

For More Information

Books

Avinesh: A Child Of The Ganges. Children of the World (series). Jean-Charles Rey (Blackbirch Press)

India. Festivals of the World (series). Falaq Kagda and Elizabeth Berg (Gareth Stevens)

India. Let's Investigate (series). Adele Richardson (Creative Education)

We're From India. Heinemann First Library (series). Victoria Parker (Heinemann Library)

Web Sites

Welcome to India
home.freeuk.net/elloughton13/india.htm
Follow a cartoon family as they explore different parts of India

Pitara Kids
www.pitara.com/magazine/features.asp
Click on various sites to read stories about India

Publisher's note to educators and parents: Our editors have carefully reviewed these Web sites to ensure that they are suitable for children. Many Web sites change frequently, however, and we cannot guarantee that a site's future contents will continue to meet our high standards of quality and educational value. Be advised that children should be closely supervised whenever they access the Internet.

Index

About the Author

Valerie Weber lives in Milwaukee, Wisconsin, with her husband and two daughters. She has been writing for children and adults for more than twenty-five years. She is grateful to both her family and friends for their support over that time. She would also like to thank the families who allowed her a glimpse of their lives for this series.